PARIS

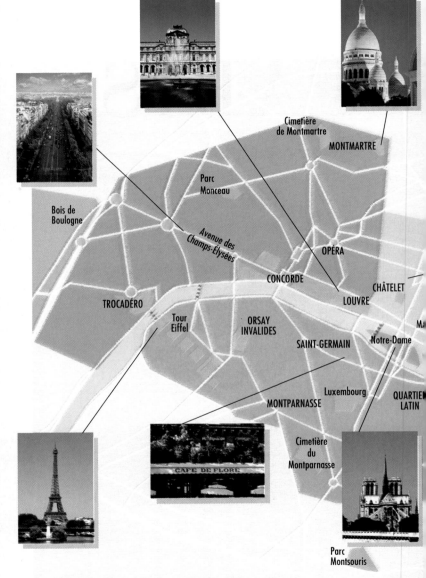

Cimetière
de Montmartre

MONTMARTRE

Parc
Monceau

Bois de
Boulogne

Avenue des
Champs-Élysées

OPÉRA

CONCORDE

CHÂTELET

TROCADÉRO

LOUVRE

Tour
Eiffel

ORSAY
INVALIDES

SAINT-GERMAIN

Notre-Dame

M

Luxembourg

QUARTIER
LATIN

MONTPARNASSE

CAFÉ DE FLORE

Cimetière
du
Montparnasse

Parc
Montsouris

0   400 m

LA VILLETTE

Parc des
Buttes-Chaumont

BELLEVILLE

Cimetière
du
Père Lachaise

BASTILLE

BERCY

Bois de
Vincennes

Blue skies over Paris. The river boat on the Seine, the roofs, the bridges and the Eiffel Tower in the distance are all unmistakable symbols of the 'City of Light'.

The history of Paris began on the banks of the Seine where the river and its many bridges encourage the visitor to stroll and explore the French capital.

A view from the banks of the Seine.

Paris and the Seine

Paris, probably more than any other capital in the world, represents the quintessential European city for those who visit it. In the words of Victor Hugo: 'More important to Europe than its people is its city, and that city is Paris'. In the same vein, it could be argued that, more important than its various districts is Paris' river and the name of that river is the Seine. The Seine flows for nearly 8 miles (13 kilometres) across Paris, and with it flow the dreams and hopes of all, including those of the artists of Montmartre (left).

The Seine, the Pont Royal and the towers of Notre-Dame-de-Paris.

The Parisian Coat of Arms and motto, Fluctuat nec mergitur, which means 'it is battered by the waves but does not flounder'.

Parisians find the Seine enchanting. Its quays are the perfect place for quiet walks or romantic strolls, and along both the *rive gauche* (Left Bank) and the *rive droite* (Right Bank), contrasting and grandiose diverse architecture and monuments recount the history of the city itself. Buildings and dreams are reflected in the river where 28 bridges allow the visitor to cross from one bank to the other without breaking the spell.

Long-standing plans for an east-west main road through Paris were finally implemented under Napoleon, when the Rue de Rivoli was extended in 1811 as far as Place de la Concorde. The buildings recall those of Bologna, Padua and Turin.

A long history

Two centuries before the birth of Christ, the Parisii, a tribe from Gaul, established itself on an island in the middle of the Seine. In 52 BC, however, the Romans conquered the island and renamed it Lutetia. Over the centuries, the city was coveted by the Huns, Barbarians and Visigoths, and finally fell into the hands of the Franks in 508 AD. Lutetia became Paris and Clovis made it his capital. A city wall was built in 1190 under Philippe-Auguste, and, in the 14th century, was extended to the Bastille. In the middle of the 19th century, Haussmann created large boulevards on the site of these fortifications. New fortifications, designed by Thiers, encompassed 11 outlying communes, thus increasing the total number of *arrondissements* from 12 to 20.

The twenty Parisian *arrondissements* (administrative districts) form a spiral around the Ile de la Cité. From the heart of this island to the outskirts, Paris, known as 'La Ville Lumière' (the 'City of Light') offers visitors a wealth of magnificent views and backdrops. Hills that were once covered in fields and vines have now been replaced by districts such as Montmartre, Belleville, the Montagne Sainte-Geneviève, Montparnasse, Passy and Chaillot. The Seine cuts through this landscape, adding to Paris' unique charm and character and providing tourists with the ideal route for discovering the city.

The Grande Arche at La Défense is a hollow cube measuring 361 feet (110 metres), coated in Carrara marble.

The Panthéon, memorial to the famous.

Dinner at the Pré Catelan, an excellent restaurant in the Bois de Boulogne, combines fine food and a pleasant setting on the outskirts of Paris.

The attractions of the beautiful Bois de Boulogne to the west of Paris include its trees, waterfalls and the two large lakes where people go to meet and sail.
Restaurants, riding centres and private clubs nestle in this oasis of greenery that lies just outside the fashionable districts of the city.

As you take time to explore Paris, you will discover many different faces of the city, from its rich historical past, symbolized by the Gothic Cathedral of Notre-Dame, the Louvre and the Panthéon, to a city of natural beauty, as seen in the Bois de Boulogne and finally the ultra-modern Paris of the Grande Arche at La Défense and the Cité des Sciences at La Villette.

The Pont des Arts footbridge, built between 1802 and 1804, was Paris' first cast-iron bridge. It was restored in 1982 and links the Institut de France with the Louvre.

The Pont-Neuf has been dubbed 'the beating heart of Paris'.

The Pont des Arts was reopened on May 22, 1984, and is a popular picnic spot in summer. On the nearby quays, the green boxes of the bouquinistes (sellers of second-hand books) sell etchings and postcards as well as books.

The somewhat ironically named **Pont-Neuf** (New Bridge) is Paris' oldest standing bridge, completed in 1606 under Henri IV. It was the first bridge to be built without buildings on it, and quickly became the haunt of artisans, teeth-pullers, cabaret singers, prostitutes, curious onlookers and pickpockets. It has always fascinated poets and artists, such as the flamboyant Christo, who wrapped the Pont-Neuf in canvas in 1985.

The majestic Pont du Carrousel dates from 1834.

Until 1632, the only way of travelling between Saint-Germain and the Palais des Tuileries (Tuileries Palace) was by ferry. A bridge was built but did not withstand flood waters for very long. The Pont Royal was constructed between 1685 and 1689 following plans drawn up by Jules Hardouin-Mansart. Its name originates from the fact that King Louis XIV personally financed all the work. Like the Pont-Neuf, the bridge has no buildings and is lined with iron lantern posts. Louis-Philippe survived two assassination attempts in front of this bridge in 1832 and 1836.

The beautiful façades of Berthillon's on the Ile Saint-Louis conceal one of the best ice cream parlours in Paris. Where better to take a break from a sightseeing trip of the island?

River boats in front of the Grand Palais.

One of the best ways to visit Paris is to take one of the *bateaux-mouches* (river boats) that sail up and down the Seine. The river is the ideal vantage point to admire many of the city's buildings and monuments and is often the focus of public festivities. On the evening of July 14, crowds gather on the bridges to watch the firework display.

Living on a péniche (narrow boat) in Paris is something of a luxury since it is relatively expensive to dock along the banks of the Seine. For those who are not fortunate enough to own one, these floating houses can be admired from the quay-sides. You may even spot the odd celebrity: the actor Jean Marais was one of the first Parisians to live on the Seine.

Paris has its own Statue of Liberty...

...the figurehead at the tip of the Ile aux Cygnes is the smaller prototype of New York's Statue of Liberty, made by Bartholdi.

The Musée de la Sculpture de Plein Air (Open-air Sculpture Museum) is on Quai Saint-Bernard, the former Port aux Vins (wine port). The park is open to the public all year round.

Tsar Nicholas II, son of Alexander III, and the French President, Félix Faure, laid the first stone of the **Pont Alexandre-III** in October 1896. It took the engineers Résal and d'Alby just two years to build the steel bridge, opened during the 1900 Universal Exhibition. From the bridge, there are views of the Champs-Elysées and the Invalides.

The 358 feet (109 metres) of the Pont Alexandre-III are decorated with shells, crustaceans and cherubs. The decoration of the four pylons supporting the single-span steel arch of the bridge symbolizes periods from the history of France.

A jewel of Gothic architecture. Notre-Dame's twin towers and high spire rise above the south-east end of the Ile de la Cité.

The banks of the Ile de la Cité and the Ile Saint-Louis are steeped in history and are full of architectural delights for the visitor to discover.

A statue of Charlemagne.

The Islands of the Seine

The Portal of the Virgin, with its relief sculptures, is one of three on Notre-Dame's main façade. Above the Virgin Mary are three kings and three prophets.

The west façade's rose window depicts Vices and Virtues, with the Virgin in the centre.

Notre-Dame Cathedral

The Cathedral of Notre Dame stands proudly in the heart of the Ile de la Cité. Ever since the 14th century, this masterpiece of faith and Gothic art has been universally influential from both an architectural and spiritual point of view.

The menacing gargoyles in the shape of demons and dragons carved into Notre-Dame's two square towers stand guard. They have not, however, been able to prevent some from desecrating the church, especially during the time of the Revolution.

Notre-Dame's high-vaulted central nave houses the Cliquot organ.

In 1160, Bishop Maurice de Sully decided to endow Paris with a cathedral that was worthy of a capital city and in 1163, Pope Alexander III laid the first stone. The building, however, was not completed until 170 years later. The creativity

Notre-Dame is also the symbolic centre of the routes linking Paris with the other towns in France. The location of the ancient city on the banks of the river led to its meteoric development.

of the builders is evident both inside and outside: the western façade, the central nave, the richly decorated chapels and the apsidal end (above) still bear witness to their genius.

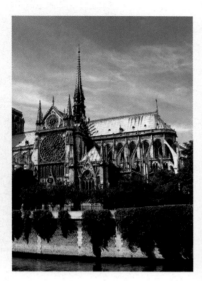

Notre-Dame's south side is adorned with spectacular medieval flying buttresses and the spire erected by Viollet-le-Duc in the 19th century. As darkness falls, the façade is floodlit, accentuating the building's Gothic architecture.

Notre-Dame through the ages

The most important events during the reigns of French monarchs were celebrated in Notre-Dame. Their weddings and funerals were held within its beautiful walls, and in 1270, St Louis' coffin was brought to the cathedral from Tunis. In 1660, the wedding of Louis XIV was celebrated here in great style. Napoleon's coronation took place in Notre-Dame on December 2, 1804, and his son, crowned King of Rome, was baptized there in 1811. In August 1944, Notre-Dame witnessed the struggle to liberate Paris from German occupation and when General de Gaulle died in 1970 a requiem mass was celebrated there. More recently, a memorial service was held following the death of President Mitterrand.

Set in the heart of 'the parish of France's history', **Notre-Dame** is one of Paris' most popular monuments. People visit it to learn about history, to pray to the Virgin Mary or simply to admire the restored architecture of the building. The fittest visitors climb the 387 steps to the top of the North Tower to admire the breathtaking view over Paris. The south tower is home to the famous Emmanuel bell, which weighs some 13 tonnes. As it calls the faithful to prayer, it conjures up pictures of Quasimodo from *The Hunchback of Notre-Dame*, a novel by Victor Hugo.

This Pietà by Nicolas Coustou, which is behind the high altar, is the centrepiece of the choir of Notre-Dame.

Notre-Dame Museum was founded in 1951 by the Friends of the Cathedral and contains several engravings, paintings and Gallo-Roman objects, as well as a 4th-century glass cup, the oldest Christian relic ever found in Paris.

Religious visitors are invited to burn candles to ask God to hear their prayers. The light from the candles and stained-glass windows creates a calm, serene atmosphere of religious devotion conducive to a visit of the cathedral's beautiful chapels and lofty nave.

The Statue of the Virgin and Child.

Inside the cathedral, the exuberant decor of the 29 chapels around the central nave and apse is breathtaking, decorated by the finest 17th-century painters, such as Le Brun. The Statue of the Virgin and Child, known as 'Notre-Dame de Paris' (Our Lady of Paris), incited the religious fervour that is described in Victor Hugo's novel of the same name.

Costou's Pietà, surrounded by six angels carrying the instruments of the Passion. On its right stands the statue of Louis XIII, and on its left, that of Louis XIV.

The shady Square du Vert-Galant on the western tip of the Ile de la Cité offers spectacular views of the Louvre and the dome of the Institut de France.

The Conciergerie with the Tour de César, the Tour d'Argent and the Tour Bonbec.

La Cité and the Ile Saint-Louis

The Ile de la Cité has long been the centre of power and is the oldest inhabited area of the city. Its smaller neighbour, originally called the Ile Notre-Dame, was renamed

The Ile de la Cité was first developed under Henri IV, with the creation of Place Dauphine to the west of the island. François Lemot's equestrian statue of King Henri (left) stands in the centre of the Pont-Neuf. It was he who named the bridge in 1606.

the Ile Saint-Louis when the king left for the Eighth Crusade.

Place Dauphine is popular with pétanque players (a game similar to boules) and those seeking a quiet place for a stroll.

Arched façades in brick and white stone are just one of the many charms this square on the tip of the Ile de la Cité has to offer.

The magnificent Place Dauphine was created to enable 'bankers and merchants to do business more easily outside the Palais'. It features frequently in the works of writers such as Nerval, Anatole France and Georges Simenon, and with its restaurants and art galleries, is still one of the most pleasant squares in Paris.

The entrance to the Sainte-Chapelle.

The triangular **Place Dauphine** was laid out under Henri IV who, in 1607, granted the land to Achille de Harlay, the first president of the Parliament. The square itself is named after the Dauphin (heir to the throne), the future Louis XIII. Within the courtyard of the nearby Palais de Justice is the **Sainte-Chapelle**, built by Louis IX to house the relics of Christ.

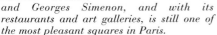

The Upper Chapel's huge stained-glass windows depict scenes from the Old and New Testaments.

Although the historical aspect of the islands has been preserved, modern cafés and restaurants provide welcome resting spots for tourists.

Heloïse and Abelard, the famous 12th century lovers, lived at 9–11 Quai aux Fleurs. Their tragic story still fascinates lovers of romance.

The market of the Quai aux Fleurs, on the small Place Louis-Lépine, offers a wide variety of plants and beautiful flowers. It is said that during the Revolution, a brave warden from

Light and shade on the Ile Saint-Louis.

Until the end of the Ancien Régime (which ended with the Revolution of 1789), religious and civil functions were centred around the Ile de la Cité. Today, Notre-Dame, the Palais de Justice, the Hôtel-Dieu (a hospital), the police headquarters and the commercial courts all still bear witness to the important role once played by this island. On Place

the Conciergerie even purchased carnations there to decorate the cell of Queen Marie-Antoinette before she was beheaded.

Flowers and plants give the balconies of the islands a peaceful village-like air.

Louis-Lépine, the **flower and bird market** is a riot of colourful blooms and feathers. While the former prison of the **Conciergerie** (the medieval part of the Palais de Justice), on the Ile de la Cité, recalls the terror of the Revolution, the quiet streets of the Ile Saint-Louis were spared the violence of political unrest.

The numerous cafés and restaurants on the Ile de la Cité and the Ile Saint-Louis create a lively atmosphere. In summer, pavement cafés spring up along the mainly pedestrianized streets where tourists while away the time under their parasols. Some, however, may prefer the extremely busy Brasserie de l'Ile-Saint-Louis, on Quai de Bourbon.

27

The Hôtel de Sully, in the Marais. One of the eight statues in bas-relief on its beautiful façades that represent the Elements and the Seasons.

A way from the islands, there is another city centre to discover, from Les Halles and the Marais, to Place de la Bastille.

A musical note in Les Halles.

Central Paris

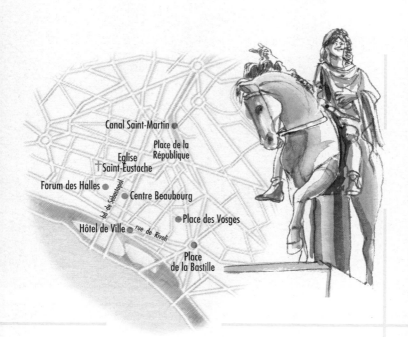

Canal Saint-Martin

Place de la République

Eglise Saint-Eustache

Forum des Halles

bd de Sébastopol

Centre Beaubourg

Place des Vosges

Hôtel de Ville

rue de Rivoli

Place de la Bastille

Colour and movement at the Igor Stravinsky Fountain, near Beaubourg. This creation by Jean Tinguely and Niki de Saint-Phalle is a tribute to the great Russian musician.

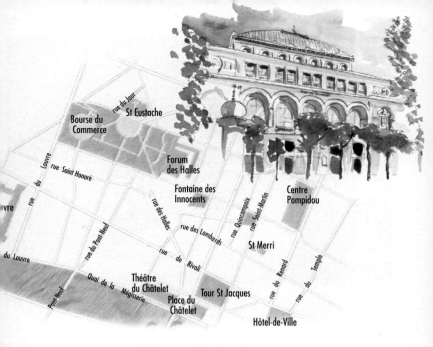

Bourse du Commerce
St Eustache
rue du Jour
rue Saint Honoré
rue du Louvre
Forum des Halles
Fontaine des Innocents
rue des Halles
rue des Lombards
rue Quincampoix
rue Saint-Martin
Centre Pompidou
St Merri
rue du Pont-Neuf
rue de Rivoli
du Louvre
rue du Renard
rue du Temple
Pont-Neuf
Quai de la Mégisserie
Théâtre du Châtelet
Place du Châtelet
Tour St Jacques
Hôtel-de-Ville

Les Halles

For almost seven centuries, Paris' main food market was in the heart of the bustling district of Les Halles. At the end of the 19th century, the writer Emile Zola rightly dubbed it 'le ventre de Paris' (the belly of Paris).

This boulangerie (bakery) sign advertises a particular French speciality: the croissant. Also available in cafés, the croissant is eaten for breakfast, or as a snack, with jam and butter or as it comes.

The glass roofs of the Forum des Halles, supported by white metal frames.

The glass roofs of the Forum des Halles, by the architects Vasconi and Pencréa'ch, blend perfectly with the gardens designed by the Lalannes, Claude and François-Xavier. This park is intended to represent the four seasons: flowers

and greenery to welcome spring and summer, Virginia creeper for autumn and stone and metal for the cold of winter.

In 1969, the fruit and vegetable market of Les Halles was moved to Rungis, in the south of the city, and replaced by a huge underground commercial and cultural centre known as the **Forum des Halles** (completed in 1979). Each day, thousands of people visit the pedestrianized area which is also a major public transport intersection.

The majestic façade of Saint-Eustache.

There are many pavement cafés and restaurants in Les Halles. They are especially busy in the evening, when people come to listen to rock and jazz bands.

Escape the hustle and bustle of the district by visiting the peaceful Fontaine des Innocents.

The **Fontaine des Innocents** (Fountain of the Innocent), nearby, is a handy meeting place and is very popular with young people. Beside the Forum, in Rue du Jour, the beautiful Church of **Saint-Eustache** was built between 1532 and 1637 and modelled on Notre-Dame. People visit the church to pray to St Rita, the patron saint of hopeless cases.

The Fontaine des Innocents, built in 1549 by Jean Goujon, symbolizes the spirit of the Renaissance. The beauty and grace of the bas-relief nymphs help the visitor to forget the presence of death that once pervaded the square. The cemetery, which once stood on this spot, was turned into a square in 1858.

The tubes on the outside of the Centre Pompidou contain escalators.

The Brancusi Studio, on Place Beaubourg, houses the works of the Romanian artist who died in 1957.

Made of metal and glass, the Centre Pompidou is 525 feet (160 m) long, 197 feet (60 m) wide, and 138 feet (42 m) tall.

It is impossible to miss the enormous brightly-coloured building covered in piping alongside the Forum des Halles. The **Centre Georges Pompidou** (Pompidou Centre), designed by Renzo Piano, Gianfranco Franchini and Richard Rogers and named after the President who commissioned it in 1970, is a national centre for art and culture. Also known as Beaubourg, its five floors contain a public library and a modern art museum.

The modern art museum houses works by artists such as Matisse, Picasso, Kandinsky and Braque. This painting by Chagall, however, remains in the Opéra.

The actress Sarah Bernhardt bought the Théâtre de la Ville in 1899.

The animated **Place du Châtelet** marks the geographical centre of Paris. Two theatres face each other on the square, namely the **Théâtre Musical de Paris** and the **Théâtre de la Ville**, both of which host concerts, operas, ballets, musicals and recitals. From the square, you can see the Gothic Tour Saint-Jacques (St Jacques Tower), dating from 1522, and, across the Seine, the towers of the Palais de Justice.

The Châtelet district is dominated by the imposing Gothic Tour Saint-Jacques. The tower is all that remains of an ancient church that was destroyed after the Revolution.

The former Place de Grève has provided the backdrop to both happy and tragic events. Over the centuries, it has witnessed many celebrations, uprisings and beheadings.

From Saint Louis to the Liberation

In 1246, King Louis IX (also known as Saint Louis) established the first municipal council. From this council of aldermen, the water merchants elected their representatives, the leader of whom was called the 'merchants' provost'. Their seal, with its famous boat, gradually became part of the coat of arms of the city of Paris, along with the motto, *Fluctuat nec mergitur*. In 1357, the merchants' provost, Etienne Marcel, purchased a large building on the Place de Grève (the Maison aux Piliers) for municipal meetings. This then became the Hôtel de Ville. More recently, this symbolic building was the headquarters of the Resistance during the liberation of Paris in August 1944.

Next to the Tour Saint-Jacques, the **Hôtel de Ville** (town hall) sits on a vast pedestrianized square, the former Place de Grève, which these days is adorned with large fountains. After the building was torched by the Communards in 1871, the central neo-Renaissance façade was faithfully reconstructed, and extended by 72 feet (22 metres). Almost 150 statues representing the towns of France, allegories and famous men and women decorate the façades of the building. It is still the centre of Paris' municipal government and receptions continue to be held in its Salle des Fêtes.

Place des Vosges in the heart of the Marais is a square surrounded by 36 brick and stone houses over a colonnade filled with cafés, antique shops and art galleries.

The charming little Square Georges-Cain beside the Musée Carnavalet.

The Marais

Built on what was once marshland on the Right Bank, north of the Ile Saint-Louis, the Marais is home to the magnificent Place des Vosges with its beautiful Renaissance buildings as well as a wealth of museums and other treasures.

The souvenir shops, cafés and restaurants under the large vaulted colonnade of Place des Vosges welcome a wide variety of visitors all year round. The famous Guirlande de Julie is a fine restaurant that is a particular favourite of meat lovers.

Place des Vosges: a tranquil and elegant spot, ideal for a romantic rendezvous.

In 1605, Henri IV ordered a vast royal square to be built, the first in Paris. It was to be surrounded with identical slate-roofed houses. The square, which occupied the site of the Hôtel des Tournelles, soon became one of the favourite

Above: A detail from the arcades surrounding Place des Vosges, still immaculate after almost 400 years. Left: One of the entrances to the royal square.

places of Parisians out for a stroll, and remains so even today. The Place Royale was renamed **Place des Vosges** in 1800 after the first region of France to pay its taxes.

A fountain on Place des Vosges. Cortot and Dupaty's equestrian statue of Louis XIII that stands in the centre of the square was likened by Victor Hugo to a 'large white ghost'.

Henri IV in Paris

Henri IV is sometimes considered to have been the first Parisian town planner. When he arrived in the capital in 1594, he intended to make it 'his town', namely, 'a world in itself and one of the world's miracles'. The Palais du Louvre was the first to benefit, and work on the Pont-Neuf began again with one major innovation: the king decided that houses would no longer be built on bridges. The two Parisian royal squares, the current Place Dauphine and Place des Vosges, are also the fruits of his labours. His greatest concern, however, was the upkeep of the city and it was he who instigated the first refuse collection service. It is for these reasons, that Henri IV has been called a pioneer.

Place des Vosges is 460 feet (140 metres) long on each side, three of which have arcades filled with shops. In the 17th century, duels took place in its central gardens, laid out under Louis XIV for people living around the square. In 1905, the gardens were open to the public. Over the years, the square has been home to Paris' most eminent families. The famous literary hostess, Madame de Sévigné, was born at No. 1b, while Victor Hugo lived at No. 6 for a time, in the Hôtel Rohan-Guéménée which is now a museum devoted to the writer.

The charms of the Marais include its distinctive town houses and attractive shops, such as the clothes boutique pictured above.

In the centre of the courtyard of the Musée Carnavalet is a statue of Louis XIV by Coysevox, which used to stand at the Hôtel de Ville.

The entrance to the museum, at 23, Rue de Sévigné. It is made up of the Hôtel Carnavalet, where Madame de Sévigné lived between 1677 and 1696, and the Hôtel Le Peletier de Saint-Fargeau. The museum is now devoted to the capital's history, from Roman times to the present day.

A tranquil side street in the Marais.

From the 14th century, the Marais became very popular with the Parisian nobility and bourgeoisie, of which the beautiful and distinctive town houses are a legacy. Most are now museums, such as the **Musée Carnavalet** (Carnavalet Museum), devoted to the history of the French capital. The area also has many clothes shops.

Square Georges-Cain, accessible from Rue Payenne, is surrounded by the Orangery, (pictured above), and the façade of the Hôtel Saint-Fargeau.

This hand-painted gilt shop sign is one of the many treasures that the Marais has to offer.

The area around Place du Marché Sainte-Catherine, near the Hôtel de Sully, is famous for its restaurants.

Enjoy a stroll in the area surrounding the Musée Picasso. The houses on the even-numbered side of Rue des Coutures Saint-Gervais, which was laid out in 1620, date from around that era. At No. 1, Rue de la Perle is the Musée Bricard which has an unusual collection of old locks and door knockers.

The entrance to the Hôtel Libéral-Bruant.

On leaving the Musée Carnavalet, the visitor arrives at the entrance to the Musée Bricard in the **Hôtel Libéral-Bruant** which is named after the architect who designed the Invalides. In the Hôtel Salé, the Musée Picasso (Picasso Museum), houses a collection that includes major works from the artist's blue, pink and Cubist periods.

The Hôtel de Sully's main courtyard, with its beautiful façades.

In the centre of the Marais, the Bibliothèque Historique de la Ville holds more than one million books on the history of Paris. Near Place des Vosges, the Hôtel de Sully, bought by the Duc de Sully in 1634, is now home to the Caisse Nationale des Monuments historiques (National Centre for Historic Monuments).

Among the stone buildings and their exuberant decor, the visitor will also find that the Marais has a certain village-like atmosphere. Here, in a shady cul-de-sac, the quiet, coolness and discreet luxury give the district its unique character. The mixture of both understated modesty and aristocratic pomp is appreciated by residents and visitors alike.

The main courtyard of the Hôtel Soubise.

The visitor can find tasty felafels and smoked salmon in the Jewish quarter, near the Hôtel de Sens (right).

There are many kosher shops and restaurants in the district's picturesque little streets. The most well-known, Rue des Rosiers, used to be a covered way.

Since 1808, the **Archives Nationales** (French National Archives) have been housed in the elegant and luxurious Hôtel de Rohan and the Hôtel Soubise, and have given their name to this part of the district. In 1712, the owner, Hercule Mériadec de Rohan, redecorated the interior to please his new young wife. Today the country's archives are so numerous that they are also housed in various other buildings around Paris.

The Hôtel de Sens, built as a fortified house, has a beautiful interior courtyard.

Back in the district of Saint-Paul, in the south-west of the Marais, is the Church of **Saint-Paul-Saint-Louis**, on Rue Saint-Antoine, one of Paris' Jesuit-style buildings. The church, which was financed by Louis XIII, is a symbol of the power of the Jesuits. The **Hôtel de Sens**, near the banks of the Seine, on the other hand, is a fine example of medieval fortified architecture. Queen Margaret of Valois, the former wife of Henri IV, lived there, transforming the citadel into a place of debauchery. The buildings now house the Bibliothèque Forney (Forney Library), founded in 1886.

No visitor should leave the Marais without visiting one of the district's tea shops. The most famous is without doubt Mariage Frères, 30, Rue du Bourg-Tibourg, not far from the Hôtel de Ville. This veritable institution is decorated in fine colonial style and sells teas from all over the world. Tea lovers are invited to sample the various blends in a setting filled with exotic aromas.

47

Perched on its globe, the Génie de la Liberté (Genius of Liberty) is a gilded statue by Augustin Dumont on top of the Colonne de Juillet in Place de la Bastille.

The welcoming terrace of a café-restaurant on Place de la Bastille.

The Bastille and the Saint-Martin Canal

The very mention of the name Bastille evokes the events that led to the creation of the Republic. Today, visitors will discover a young fashionable district, between the

The area around the Bastille is very different from what it was like during the days of the Revolution. Now popular with the young, it has become a fashionable meeting place thanks to its many restaurants and bistrots.

Port de l'Arsenal in the south and the Saint-Martin Canal in the north.

The Bastille was built under King Charles V and completed in 1380 to prevent invasions from the east. The fortress, however, is better-known as a famous prison and symbol of royal despotism in 1789. The building no longer exists, and Place de la Bastille now occupies the site.

If you want to take your mind off the Revolution, stop off at Les Phares, a pleasant café on the square, where the conversation ranges from philosophy to a variety of other topics.

Right: A statue of one of the key figures of the Revolution, Cambacérès, who approved the beheading of King Louis XVI. The severe face of the man who also contributed to the writing of the French Civil Code should not, however, dissuade visitors from heading towards the Arsenal in search of other treasures.

The marina of the Bassin de l'Arsenal.

On July 14, 1789, the storming of the **Bastille** brought to an end the tyrannical power of the monarchy and heralded the beginning of the French Revolution. Later, in 1833, a hollow bronze column (the Colonne de Juillet) was erected in the middle of the square as a memorial to the victims who died during the Revolution of July 1830.

To mark the bicentenary of the Revolution, the government commissioned the
enormous glass, metal and stone Opéra-Bastille, designed by Carlos Ott.

A workshop in one of the hidden alleys off Faubourg Saint-Antoine.

Leave the square and sombre thoughts of the Revolution behind you and turn onto Rue du Faubourg Saint-Antoine. This busy wide thoroughfare, linking Place de la Bastille to Place de la Nation, was once the preserve of furniture makers. Today, this tradition lives on in the shops, where cabinetmakers and inlayers ply their trade making sofas, armchairs and tables in a mixture of antique styles.

To discover a different side of the Bastille district, simply turn into any of the courtyards and lanes hidden behind the buildings of Rue de Faubourg Saint Antoine.

Far from the madding crowd, lose yourself in a maze of lanes and alleys. This leafy sun-kissed pathway presents a more rural face of Paris.

International shows

The imposing Opéra National de la Bastille, dedicated to opera, has a seating capacity of 2700. In spite of its tumultuous beginnings, when management problems led to the dismissal of several directors, the Bastille Opera today stages performances that are renowned the world over. It is, however, not the only cultural attraction in the area. Those with more cinematographic interests have the choice of several cinemas, whilst theatre-goers are catered for at the Théâtre de la Bastille in Rue de la Roquette. Further on, on Boulevard Voltaire, pop and rock fans can see their heroes at the Bataclan, one of the capital's most famous venues for concerts.

The exponents of another craft have also recently moved to the area. For the past ten or so years, many artists have taken up residence in abandoned warehouses that have now been converted into apartments. These new inhabitants have rejuvenated the Bastille, and made it into the creative and trendy area that it is today. The traditional bistros that are part of Paris' charm are once again full, particularly in the evenings. The bars and clubs along Rue de Lappe and Rue de la Roquette attract a night-time clientele whose tastes vary from the waltz and the accordion to techno music.

One of the many footbridges spanning the Saint-Martin Canal.

Near the Saint-Martin Canal, the Hôpital Saint-Louis is one of the very finest examples of early 17th-century architecture. The brick and stone building was founded by Henri IV and built between 1607 and 1611 by Claude Vellefaux.

Along the north end of Boulevard Richard Lenoir is the **Saint-Martin Canal**. With its locks and iron footbridges, the canal has retained all of its charm that was so dear to the actress Arletty, who starred opposite Louis Jouvet in the film *Hôtel du Nord*. The hotel itself can still be seen at No. 101 Quai de Jemmapes, standing on the banks of the canal in an area that has now been classified as a site of historical interest.

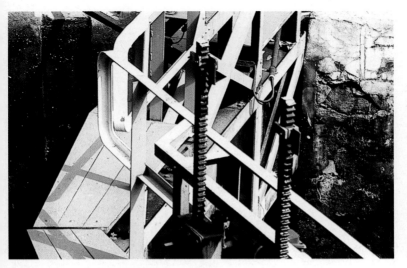

The opening and closing of the locks is quite a spectacle.

The Saint-Martin Canal, which was opened in 1825, flows into the Seine. At the start of the century, the population of the district was mainly working-class and today it still retains an air of imperturbable nonchalance. The canal, which is 3 miles (5 kilometres) long, is used mainly by barges and pleasure boats that dock in the Port de l'Arsenal. Although it is near République and the Bastille, Saint-Martin remains somewhat isolated, a place where tourists can enjoy a pleasant stroll through an area that is gradually divesting itself of its poverty and industrial past.

On the wide Boulevard Richard-Lenoir, not far from the Saint-Martin Canal, people often enjoy a game of pétanque. Visitors can also enjoy a drink or meal on the Quai de Jemmapes, at the La Marine bar-restaurant.

The Chapelle Sainte-Ursule at the Sorbonne University. It was built between 1635 and 1642, and houses the tomb of Cardinal Richelieu, sculpted by Girardon.

From the Latin Quarter to the Eiffel Tower, via the cafés of Saint-Germain-des-Prés the Left Bank of the Seine retains a particularly Parisian charm.

The Fontaine Saint-Michel.

The Left Bank

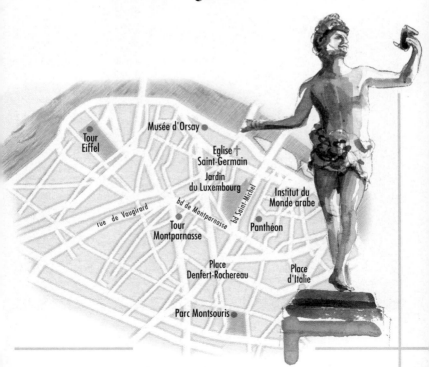

Tour Eiffel

Musée d'Orsay

Eglise Saint-Germain

Jardin du Luxembourg

Institut du Monde arabe

bd de Montparnasse

bd Saint-Michel

rue de Vaugirard

Tour Montparnasse

Panthéon

Place Denfert-Rochereau

Place d'Italie

Parc Montsouris

The Fontaine Saint-Michel by Davioud (1860). In the central niche is Duret's statue of St Michael slaying the dragon, inspired by a painting by Raphael.

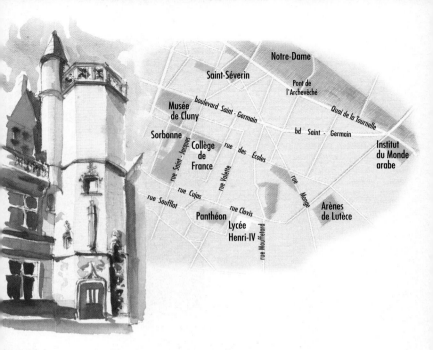

Notre-Dame
Saint-Séverin
Pont de l'Archevêché
boulevard Saint - Germain
Musée de Cluny
Quai de la Tournelle
bd Saint - Germain
Sorbonne
Collège de France
rue des Écoles
rue Saint - Jacques
Institut du Monde arabe
rue Valette
rue Cujas
rue Souflot
rue Clovis
Panthéon
Lycée Henri-IV
rue Mouffetard
rue Monge
Arènes de Lutèce

The Latin Quarter

The Latin Quarter was, and still is, the preserve of students and intellectuals. Since the Sorbonne opened in the 13th century, it has been an important centre of learning in the midst of prestigious colleges and secondary schools.

The Latin Quarter has always been associated with free-thinking and liberty since the French philosopher Abélard settled on the Left Bank of the Seine in the 12th century, having been banished from Notre-Dame.
The area was also the backdrop for the events of May 1968, which rocked the whole of France.

The Panthéon houses more than 60 tombs of illustrious French people. Jean Moulin, who died in 1943 and represents the spirit of the Resistance, has been buried there since 1964. Writers, however, are the most heavily represented group. Among the most famous to be buried in this secularized temple are Victor Hugo, Emile Zola, Jean-Jacques Rousseau and Voltaire. Politicians, such as Jean Jaurès, and scientists are also buried here, and have recently been joined by the two winners of the Nobel Prize for Physics, Pierre and Marie Curie.

A florist's shop on Rue de Médicis.

As you walk up Boulevard Saint-Michel from the Seine, you will come across the Musée de Cluny. This 16th-century building houses treasures, such as the Dame à la Licorne *(Lady with the Unicorn) tapestries, Renaissance illuminated manuscripts and many other rare objects.*

East of Boulevard Saint-Michel, the **Panthéon** stands on the Montagne Sainte-Geneviève. This neoclassical building was designed by the architect Soufflot, and is built on the site of the former Church of Sainte-Geneviève. Completed in 1790, ten years after Soufflot's death, the church was turned into a pantheon for the nation's greatest citizens.

This view of the Panthéon, at the end of Rue Soufflot, is from the fountain on Place Edmond-Rostand, in front of the entrance to the Jardin du Luxembourg.

The Arènes de Lutèce formed the largest known amphitheatre in Gaul.

The Institut du Monde Arabe was founded in 1980 as a joint venture between France and around 20 Arab countries and is housed in a building that was designed by Jean Nouvel.
The institute covers Muslim civilization from the seventh century to the present day.

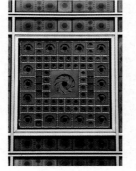

After a rest in the Jardin du Luxembourg (Luxembourg Gardens), turn into Rue Soufflot and pass through the narrow streets behind the Panthéon into Rue Mouffetard. This district is full of theatres, cinemas, bookshops, cafés and restaurants. You will then come to the amphitheatre of the Arènes de Lutèce, and, if you turn back towards the Seine, the **Institut du Monde Arabe** (Arabic Institute).

In summer, the restaurants lining Rue Mouffetard spill out onto the pavement.

An open-air market stands in the partly pedestrianized Rue Mouffetard. It is one of the oldest in Paris and popular with those who live in the quarter (which is also called the 'Mouffe'). **Place de la Contrescarpe**, at the junction with Rue Lacépède, is lined with restaurants and cafés, adding to the lively atmosphere of the market. Next, take Rue de Navarre on the left, towards the Gallo-Roman ruins of the **Arènes de Lutèce** (Arena of Lutetia). The site was excavated in 1869 and is today used for football and *pétanque* matches (a game similar to boules).

The Jardin des Plantes (Botanical Gardens), which is accessible from Rue Geoffroy-Saint-Hilaire, was founded in 1626 by two of Louis XIII's physicians. Not to be missed are 2600 types of medicinal and edible plants, more than 2000 plants from various corners of the world, greenhouses devoted to rare vegetation and species, and of course, the Musée National d'Histoire Naturel (the Natural History Museum).

The Church of Saint-Germain-des-Prés is the oldest in Paris. It stands in the square of the same name, where the famous café Les Deux Magots is situated.

Ecole des Beaux-Arts
Institut de France
Hôtel des Monnaies
rue des Saints-Pères
rue Bonaparte
rue de Seine
rue Mazarine
Café de Flore
Lipp
Musée Delacroix
rue du Dragon
bd
rue de Buci
Saint   Germain
rue de Rennes
rue Mabillon
Saint-Sulpice
rue de l'Odéon
rue Bonaparte
Théâtre de l'Odéon
rue de Vaugirard
Sénat
Jardin du Luxembourg

Saint-Germain-des-Prés and Montparnasse

The Left Bank area of Saint-Germain-des-Prés and its neighbour Montparnasse have always had an impact on writers, artists and poets. The artistic and intellectual activities

A symbol of the Left Bank immediately after World War II, the name of Saint-Germain-des-Prés stirs many a French body and soul.

Montparnasse (left) and its famous tower has also inspired a number of artists, sculptors and writers over the years.

of the districts were largely centred around their legendary cafés.

The Church of Saint-Germain dates back to Childebert, son of Clovis (6th century).

Art lovers will delight in the many galleries dotted around the district. On leaving these mini-museums, quench your thirst with a 'diabolo menthe' (mint cordial and water) or a 'kir' (white wine and crème de cassis) in one of the

Parisian cafés are friendly animated places.
Left: The Procope, founded in 1686, is the oldest café in Paris. Nowadays, it is an expensive restaurant.

famous local cafés. The best view of the Church of Saint-Germain is from the terrace of **Les Deux Magots**, once the favourite haunt of artists, philosophers and writers.

charming square lies at the bottom of Rue de Fürstenberg, next to the Church of Saint Germain. This haven of tranquillity was chosen by the artist Eugène Delacroix as the site for his studio, which is now a museum.

Saint-Sulpice, the other church

At the southern end of Saint-Germain, on the other side of the boulevard, Place Saint-Sulpice is dominated by the church of the same name. Its façade is sombre, almost austere, but the exterior hides a harmonious and spacious interior which is richly decorated. The painter, Eugène Delacroix, referred to by Baudelaire as the 'epitome of the painter-poet', decorated the famous Chapelle des Saints-Anges (Chapel of the Holy Angels), just one of the many peaceful wonders to be discovered in the light-filled church. Outside, have a drink at the quiet Café de la Mairie on the square surrounded by shops, bookstores and the town hall of the 6th *arrondissement*.

The abbey, founded around 543 by Childebert under the counsel of Saint Germain, covered a huge area, comprising several hectares of agricultural land, hence the word 'prés' (meadows) in the name **Saint-Germain-des-Prés**. To the left of the church square, Square Laurent-Prache recalls the area's rural past, and is home to a bronze sculpture of a woman's face, created by Picasso in memory of the poet Apollinaire, who frequented the Café de Flore. At the bottom of Rue de l'Abbaye, Rue de Fürstenberg leads to a charming little square of the same name.

The Café de Flore, where Jean-Paul Sartre and Simone de Beauvoir met.

As a 19-year old bachelor, Victor Hugo lived at No. 30, Rue du Dragon, a street perpendicular to the Boulevard St-Germain.

The Brasserie Lipp, founded in 1880, is the haunt of those working in broadcasting, publishing, and

politics. Its interior decor of ceramic tiles, worthy of a visit, has led it to be classified as a monument of historical interest.

The **Café de Flore**, not far from Les Deux Magots, was also frequented by post-war intellectuals, whilst the **Brasserie Lipp**, opposite, has tended to be favoured more by actors and ministers. Today, however, clothes shops detract somewhat from the intellectual and artistic ambiance that used to characterize the area.

A quaint street in Saint-Germain.

There are now many clothes shops in the area, selling both designer labels and cheaper brands, especially on and around Boulevard Saint-Germain.

Bookworms and art lovers will enjoy a visit to the second-hand bookshops and galleries along Rue Mazarine.

The nearby Rue de Buci has retained its working-class character, with its bustling market and bistros which are less exclusive than the Flore and Les Deux Magots. An important thoroughfare for centuries, it leads to the junction of Rue Mazarine and Rue Dauphine. Both streets lead to the Seine, whilst the former also leads to the Institut de France.

The Buci is a very lively café on Rue Mazarine. At No. 12 of the same street, the playwright Boizard de Ponteau, founded the Opéra-Comique in 1728, where Favart staged his first play in 1734. The Opéra-Comique, also called the Salle Favart, is now found in the area around the Opéra Garnier.

This gilded handle featuring two snakes' heads, decorates the door of the Musée de la Monnaie. This museum, at 11 Quai Conti, was founded in 1827.

Rue de l'Odéon leads towards the Théâtre de l'Europe. This neo-classical theatre has a reputation for staging quality plays and shows.

Right: The Ecole des Beaux-Arts de Paris. The prestigious college by the Seine, on Quai Malaquais, was founded in 1816 in the 18th-century Hôtel de Chimay, the former 17th-century Couvent des Petits-Augustins and several 19th-century buildings, including the Loges constructed by Debret around 1820.

A courtyard in Saint-Germain-des-Prés.

The **Ecole des Beaux-Arts**, the **Institut de France** (which is now home to the Académie Française) and the Musée de la Monnaie (Museum of the Mint) are all found on Quai Conti and Quai Malaquais. These nationally-renowned symbols of art, knowledge and wealth are the pride of the area in which Voltaire and Baudelaire once lived.

The Institut de France on Quai Conti was designed by Louis le Vau and completed in 1691. It houses five academies, including the Académie Française.

The Cemetery of Montparnasse, near Boulevard Raspail, is a large area of greenery where you can stroll among the graves of famous people. Those buried here include Maupassant, Serge Gainsbourg, Jean-Paul Sartre and Simone de Beauvoir. The tombs are often eye-catching, such as Brancusi's famous Baiser *(Kiss), which overlooks its creator's grave, and* La Douleur *(Sorrow) on the tombstone of the sculptor Henri Laurens.*

The famous café Closerie des Lilas.

Leave Saint-Germain via Rue de Rennes and head for the district of Montparnasse, the stomping ground of poets, writers, artists and sculptors. Modigliani, Picasso, Miro, Kandinski, Max Ernst and many others had studios in the area, many of them in Rue Campagne-Première, whilst the likes of Cocteau and Hemmingway visited the local cafés and cabarets.

After a coffee at the Closerie des Lilas, why not take a quiet stroll in the Jardin du Luxembourg? The gardens are filled with statues and are also home to the Fontaine de Médicis. Queen Marie de Médicis had a Florentine palace built on a site purchased from the Carthusians in 1615 to remind her of her native land. Since 1958, it has been used to house the Sénat *(French Senate).*

La Coupole in Montparnasse, where people go to eat, drink and dance.

The large brasseries, crêperies and many cinemas make **Montparnasse** one of the capital's liveliest districts. The names of some restaurants recall the fact that the area traditionally attracted large numbers of Bretons arriving in Paris to make their fortune. Today, the modern station of Montparnasse still serves western France.

Above: An art deco building on Rue Campagne-Première. The façade of the building at No. 31 was decorated by Paul Bigot.

Left: The Tour Montparnasse, made of steel and smoked glass, was completed in 1973. On the top floor, some 656 feet (200 metres) and 56 stories up in the air there is a restaurant and bar offering panoramic views of Paris.

The monuments of Paris are spectacularly floodlit in the evening. This photo shou the obelisk in Place de la Concorde in front of the Eiffel Tower.

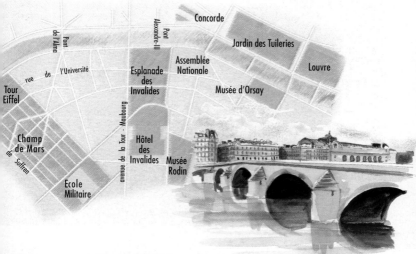

From the Musée d'Orsay to the Eiffel Tower

The Left Bank also has its share of wide open spaces. To see these, walk along the Seine from the Musée d'Orsay in the east to the Champ-de-Mars and the Eiffel Tower

A statue by Joseph Bernard, Femme et enfant dansant (Woman and Child Dancing) stands in the central hall of the Musée d'Orsay. The museum exhibits paintings, sculptures, furniture and photographs, dating from the second half of the 19th century to 1914.

in the west, crossing the large Esplanade des Invalides on the way.

The long façade conceals the Musée d'Orsay's large central hall.

Walk along Quai Anatole France, from the Ecole des Beaux-Arts to the **Musée d'Orsay** (Orsay Museum). The former station, opened during the Universal Exhibition of 1900, was about to be demolished in the 1970s, but was restored and transformed into a museum between 1980 and 1986. The museum itself exhibits art from the period between 1848 and 1914 under an enormous glass roof. The

The Gare d'Orsay (Orsay Station) designed at the turn of the century by Victor Laloux, became a temple of art in the late 19th century. Opposite, the former station clock is still in working order.

The glass roof and size of the museum provide the perfect setting in which to exhibit the collection of sculptures.

Antoine Bourdelle

The Archer, above, is a bronze statue by Bourdelle found on the middle level of the Musée d'Orsay, on one of the sculpture terraces. This Greek hero is one of the most well-known in classical mythology, and is also the work which brought fame to one of France's greatest sculptors. Antoine Bourdelle was born in Montauban in the South of France in 1861. He spent ten years as Auguste Rodin's assistant and was greatly influenced by him in his early years. *The Archer* was completed in 1909 and represents a departure from his master's style. The Musée Antoine-Bourdelle (Antoine Bourdelle Museum), close to Montparnasse Station, is housed in the studio used by the sculptor until his death in 1929.

magnificent building serves as a showcase for works that illustrate major artistic movements, such as Realism, Art Nouveau and Impressionism. Its most famous paintings include *Le Déjeuner sur l'herbe* by Manet, *La gare Saint-Lazare* by Monet, and Renoir's *Le Moulin de la Galette*. A number of other masters are also represented: the visitor can admire Cézanne's provençal light, Van Gogh's vibrant colours, Gauguin's exoticism, Degas' dancing girls and Toulouse-Lautrec's posters. The sculptures on display include Rodin's *La Porte de l'enfer* (The Gate of Hell).

On the other side of the wide Boulevard des Invalides is the Musée Rodin (Rodin Museum), which houses the major works of the sculptor who died in the 18th-century Hôtel de Biron in 1917.

The pediment and arches on the façade of the Hôtel des Invalides, which is nearly 660 feet (200 metres) long.

Right: One of the 17th and 18th-century bronze cannons found at the Invalides. This vast complex is home to several museums, including the Musée de l'Armée (Military History Museum), which retraces France's military past, built by Mansart between 1679 and 1708.

The Assemblée Nationale.

On leaving the Musée d'Orsay, pass the Assemblée Nationale (or Palais Bourbon) and you will come to the Esplanade des Invalides. Behind its long classical façade, the beautiful **Hôtel des Invalides** conceals 17 courtyards and spreads over 25 acres (10 hectares). It was commissioned by Louis XIV in 1670 to house his wounded soldiers.

In a crypt under the large gilded dome of the Invalides lies Napoleon's tomb which was designed by Joachim Visconti and took more than 20 years to construct.

The Pont d'Iéna links the Eiffel Tower and the Jardins du Trocadéro.

The lifts of the Eiffel Tower were installed at the time of its construction in 1889, now providing access to the Jules Verne restaurant. Bourdelle's statue of Eiffel, at the foot of the pillar on the north side, pays tribute to the engineer who designed this striking Parisian landmark.

The **Tour Eiffel** (Eiffel Tower) dominates the Parc du Champ-de-Mars, rising 1050 feet (320 metres) above the Seine. This tall structure is floodlit in the evening, highlighting its lacework of iron. It is a triumph of technical progress, but its engineer, Gustave Eiffel, was not simply interested in creating a wonder of technological development. He also invested time in the structure's aesthetic appeal.

The Eiffel Tower weighs a massive 9840 tons (10,000 tonnes), and offers stunning views of Paris and its outskirts from the top of its 1652 steps.

These gilded bronze statues adorning the esplanade of the Palais de Chaillot seem dwarfed by the Eiffel Tower rising on the opposite bank of the Seine.

Paris' Right Bank calls to mind not only the Arc de Triomphe and the Champs-Elysées but also the Louvre, the Opéra and Montmartre.

An aerial view of the Trocadéro.

The Right Bank

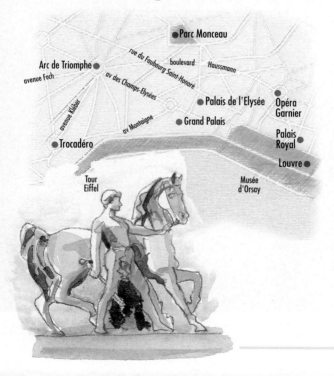

Parc Monceau

Arc de Triomphe

avenue Foch

rue du Faubourg Saint-Honoré

boulevard Haussmann

av des Champs-Elysées

avenue Kléber

av Montaigne

Palais de l'Elysée

Grand Palais

Trocadéro

Opéra Garnier

Palais Royal

Louvre

Tour Eiffel

Musée d'Orsay

The Avenue des Champs-Elysées. The haunt of tourists from all over the world but also the setting for the traditional July 14 military parade.

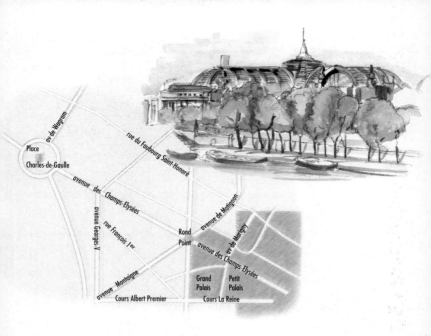

Place Charles-de-Gaulle
av. de Wagram
rue du Faubourg Saint-Honoré
avenue des Champs-Elysées
avenue Georges-V
rue François 1er
avenue Montaigne
Cours Albert Premier
Rond Point
avenue de Matignon
av. de Marigny
avenue des Champs-Elysées
Grand Palais
Petit Palais
Cours La Reine

The Champs-Elysées

To walk along the Champs-Elysées is to walk along the most beautiful avenue in the world. Once the place where society came to take the air, the avenue has since

Opposite: One of the sculptures on the pillars of the Arc de Triomphe. Here, Le Départ des Volontaires (Departure of the Volunteers), better known as La Marseillaise, was sculpted by François Rude between 1835 and 1836.

become a busy thoroughfare, lined with enticing shop windows.

The Champs-Elysées is also internationally renowned for its luxury shops. Prestigious haute couturiers have their premises in the surrounding streets: Guy Laroche, for example, has a shop on Avenue Montaigne.

Above: Also in Avenue Montaigne are the premises of another name from the world of fashion: Christian Dior.

The Champs-Elysée is still a very popular place for a stroll. The avenue, which was created in the 17th century to extend the view from Les Tuileries, attracts many tourists with its shops, cinemas, large cafés and even the fast-food outlets that now line it between the Rond-Point and the Arc de Triomphe.

The Arc de Triomphe, on Place de l'Etoile.

At the western end of the Champs-Elysées stands the **Arc de Triomphe**. Built by Napoleon I to celebrate the great victory at Austerlitz in 1805 and the glory of the Grande Armée, it has since been associated with all the major events in France's history. Under the central arch is the Tomb of the Unknown Soldier, on which burns an eternal flame.

The Rond-Point on the Champs-Elysées.

To the east, from the Rond-Point on the Champs-Elysées to Place de la Concorde, the wide thoroughfare takes on a very different character. On either side of the avenue there are many shaded gardens, museums and theatres. Nearby is the **Palais de l'Elysée** (Elysée Palace), the official residence of the President of the Republic.

The most sought-after addresses in Paris are to be found on and around the Champs-Elysées. Not content with the most famous names in haute couture and luxury goods, the area also has the most exclusive hotels (including the sumptuous Hôtel Plaza Athénée on Avenue Montaigne, above right) and the presidential palace (above left) with its elaborate entrance gates.

The Jardins du Trocadéro cover an area of 25 acres (10 hectares).

The Colline de Chaillot, to the south-west of the Jardins des Champs-Elysées (Elysian Gardens), was chosen by Napoleon I as the site for a grandiose building project and is now home to the Palais de Chaillot (Chaillot Palace), with its theatre and

The area is dotted with luxurious hôtels particuliers (town houses) such as the beautiful example shown left, set back behind trees away from the noise of the streets.

museums overlooking the Jardins du **Trocadéro** (Trocadero Gardens). Its two curved wings overlook a square decorated with bronze statues and an ornamental lake.

The façades of the Palais du Chaillot were decorated by many different sculptors and painters. Bas-reliefs stand alongside gold inscriptions by the poet Paul Valéry.

In the heart of museumland

The Colline de Chaillot greatly inspired architects from the time of Napoleon's initial development project, abandoned when the Empire fell, until the building of the current palace. The 16th *arrondissement*, surrounding this giant architectural phenomenon, also has a high concentration of museums. The Goncourt brothers rekindled an interest in 18th-century art, while Emile Guimet assembled an enormous collection of Asiatic art, which is currently on display in the museum named after him. The Marmottans, both father and son, left a rich collection of art from the First Empire, as well as numerous Impressionist paintings, including over 60 by Claude Monet.

Built by Davioud for the 1878 Universal Exhibition, the Palais du Trocadéro was remodelled by the architects Carlu, Boileau and Azéma, and was renamed the **Palais de Chaillot** for the 1937 Exhibition. It houses the **Musée de l'Homme**, a museum devoted to anthropology, ethnology and prehistory as well as the **Musée de la Marine** (Maritime Museum), the **Musée du Cinéma** (Cinema Museum) and the **Musée des Monuments Français** (Museum of French Monuments). On the same site, the **Théâtre National de Chaillot** is one of Paris' largest theatres.

The Quadriges *by Recipon adorn each corner of the Grand Palais.*

Right: The Pont Alexandre-III links the Grand Palais and Petit Palais to the classical Hôtel des Invalides. Although the Grand Palais was built as a 'monument to the glory of French art', it is, in fact, dedicated to art from around the world.

Heading east along the Seine, the visitor will arrive at the Jardins des Champs-Elysées and the **Grand Palais**. Built under Girault's guidance between 1897 and 1900, this huge metal hall with its vast glass dome is a fine example of *belle époque* architecture. The building's façades are covered in stones brought from all over France. Be warned: the exhibitions and retrospectives held at the Grand Palais often attract very long queues.

The main façade of the Petit Palais with its Ionic colonnade.

On the other side of Avenue Winston Churchill, the **Petit Palais**, which was also designed by the architect Charles Girault, is a masterpiece in stone that heralds the return to academicism. Designed at the same time as its neighbour, the Grand Palais, and the Pont Alexandre-III, it was intended to house French works of art for the 1900 Universal Exhibition. Nowadays, its galleries contain sculpture and painting collections, which, as a result of their rather disparate nature, provide an overview of the artistic treasures that Paris has acquired over the years.

The Petit Palais is closed on Monday and public holidays, but is open every other day from 10 am to 5.40 pm. It contains a charming interior courtyard and garden with ornamental lakes and sculptures by famous artists.

One of the two fountains on either side of the obelisk on Place de la Concorde. Louis XVI was guillotined on the square in 1793.

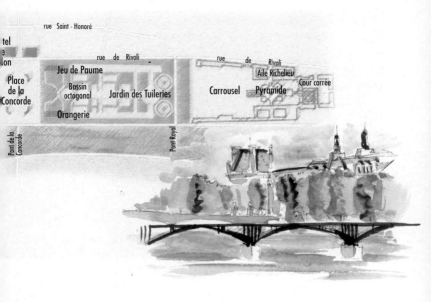

rue Saint - Honoré

Place de la Concorde

Jeu de Paume

rue de Rivoli

Bassin octogonal

Jardin des Tuileries

Orangerie

rue de Rivoli

Aile Richelieu

Carrousel

Pyramide

Cour carrée

Pont de la Concorde

Pont Royal

Concorde and the Louvre

At the opposite end from Place de l'Etoile, the most beautiful avenue in the world leads onto the most beautiful square in the world, Place de la Concorde. Further

Elegant squares, streets lined with arcades, museums and gardens give the district its d i s t i n c t i v e character. It is an area of Paris in which the power of reason reigns, as shown by the strict layout of Place de la Concorde and the formal Jardin des Tuileries.

on, the Jardin des Tuileries leads to the world's largest museum, the Louvre.

The Luxor obelisk is 75 feet (23 metres) high and nearly 3000 years old.

Place de la Concorde, covering more than 20 acres (8 hectares), offers breathtaking views of the Champs-Elysées, the Madeleine, the Tuileries and, on the other side of the Seine, the Assemblée Nationale, making it one of the most beautiful

Gabriel, the first architect to work on Place de la Concorde, was responsible for some beautiful buildings, such as the Ministère de la Marine and the Hôtel Crillon.

intersections in Paris. Standing on the site of the former Place de la Révolution, its fountains and statues are best appreciated at dawn, when Paris is waking and there is little traffic.

The fountains on the square are 29 feet (9 metres) tall, and are symbols of maritime and river navigation. They were inspired by those in St Peter's Square in Rome.

The Luxor obelisk was a gift from Mohammed-Ali Pasha to Louis-Philippe in 1831, and was erected in 1836. It is covered in hieroglyphics recounting the exploits of the pharaoh Rameses II and marks the centre of Place de la Concorde, designed by Jacques-Ange Gabriel and opened in 1763. The current layout, redesigned by the architect Hittorff, dates from 1835. The western opening onto the Avenue des Champs-Elysées is decorated with copies of Coustou's famous *Chevaux de Marly* (Marly Horses), the originals of which are now on display in the Louvre.

Famous heads on the square

During the 1789 French Revolution, the history of Plàce de la Concorde suddenly took on enormous and bloody proportions when the infamous guillotine was erected there and used to behead many people, too numerous to list. The names of some of the most important to be beheaded, however, are inscribed for posterity on plaques around the capital.

King Louis XVI, Queen Marie-Antoinette, Danton, Charlotte Corday, Camille Desmoulins, Saint-Just and Philippe Egalité were all decapitated on the former Place de la Révolution. The guillotine was moved to the current Place de la Nation for a while, but was brought back to behead Robespierre.

A statue at the main entrance to the Jardin des Tuileries.

The Musée du Jeu de Paume in the Jardin des Tuileries (right) hosts temporary modern art exhibitions.
The Musée des Arts Décoratifs (Museum of Art and Design) and the Musée des Arts de la Mode (Museum of Fashion) are on Rue de Rivoli, alongside the gardens.

The entrance to the **Jardin des Tuileries** (Tuileries Gardens) is on Place de la Concorde. Le Nôtre, Louis XIV's gardener, designed the garden's current layout in the 17th century. The entire district, with its formal gardens, museums and monuments, is a legacy from the time when France was ruled by its greatest kings. These gardens lead to the Louvre, but before visiting this unmissable palace of art, head for the

The ornamental lake in the Jardin des Tuileries.

Musée de l'Orangerie to the right of the garden's entrance. It houses the fine Walter-Guillaume collection, featuring works from 1870 to 1930, including paintings by Renoir, Cézanne, Derain, Soutine, Picasso, Matisse and Claude Monet's famous *Nymphéas* (Water Lilies) series, in a gallery described as the 'Sistine Chapel of Impressionism'. Opposite the Orangerie, the Jeu de Paume houses temporary exhibitions of contemporary works. Finally, past the Arc de Triomphe du Carrousel is the breathtaking Grand Louvre and its glass pyramid.

House martins have begun building their nests under the Arc de Triomphe du Carrousel, within sight of the Louvre. These birds, with bluish-black and white plumage on their bellies and rumps are a much rarer sight in Paris than pigeons!

Rue de Rivoli is lined with neoclassical buildings. The art galleries and fashion houses under their arches are popular with visitors to the Louvre.

Above: Frémiet's gilded bronze statue of Joan of Arc (1874) stands on Place des Pyramides near the Louvre.

The Sully wing and glass pyramid.

The Arc de Triomphe du Carrousel, inspired by the Arch of Septimus Severus in Rome, was built in coloured marble between 1806 and 1808 to celebrate Napoleon's victories of 1805. It used to form part of the entrance to the Palais des Tuileries which was demolished in 1882.

In 1981, President François Mitterrand decided to remodel and enlarge the Palais du **Louvre**. What was once a fortified wall at the time of Philippe Auguste was thus transformed into the largest museum in the world. Visitors now enter the museum through the **glass pyramid**, designed by the architect Ieoh Ming Pei and erected in 1989. Beneath

The glass pyramid stands at the entrance to the Louvre.

the pyramid lies a large arcade of shops. In the Richelieu wing, opened in 1993, Coustou's sculpture, the *Chevaux de Marly* (Marly Horses), copies of which still stand in Place de la Concorde, rear up to greet visitors, inviting them to stroll through the museum's vast galleries in search of great masterpieces.

The Kings of France lived in the Palais du Louvre for nearly four centuries. In the 16th century, François I built a Renaissance castle on the site and then provided the Louvre with its first exhibits. The king was passionate about Italian art and acquired Leonardo da Vinci's Mona Lisa *(or* La Joconde *in French), whose enigmatic smile continues to seduce visitors to the museum.*

The base of the medieval towers built in 1190 that once stood on the site of the Louvre.

To visit the Louvre is to immerse yourself in the infinite world of art. The museum first opened its doors to the public in 1793 and has continued to grow in size ever since. The visitor would now need several days to visit the whole museum. Its 420,000 works, only a selection of which are on display at any one time, retrace thousands of years of history, from Antiquity to the 19th century, via the Renaissance.

Above: The Victoire de Samothrace *is a masterpiece of Greek sculpture.*

The terrace of the prestigious Café Marly at the Louvre was designed by Olivier Gagnère and Yves Taralon.

Oriental, Egyptian, Greek, Etruscan and Roman civilizations are extremely well-represented. In one of the rooms the famous *Scribe accroupi* (Squatting Scribe) appears to be writing to Champollion whilst the spread wings of the *Victoire de Samothrace* (Winged Victory of Samothrace) point to other galleries surveyed by the beautiful *Venus de Milo*. The collection of paintings features works by many old masters. Rembrandt, Bosch, Dürer, Titian, Raphael and Goya are all represented in a collection that will provide a feast for the eyes and uplift the soul.

Celebrations at the Louvre

The Louvre has, over the years, been a fortress, a prison, a depot, a palace and a ministry, as well as the setting for lavish festivities. Ballets, carousels and masked balls were all part of everyday life at court during the 16th and 17th centuries. During such festivities, princes, princesses, courtiers and courtesans wore the most beautiful costumes. Today, the museum has retained something of this tradition by staging fashion shows in the Carrousel's large underground complex. This gallery, designed by Pei and Macary in 1993, extends from the pyramid to the Carrousel. Famous designers come to dress the world's most beautiful women a mere stone's throw away from the beauties hanging in the museum.

The grand staircase of the Opéra Garnier. Its curves, marble and lamplight set the tone for the splendour of the productions.

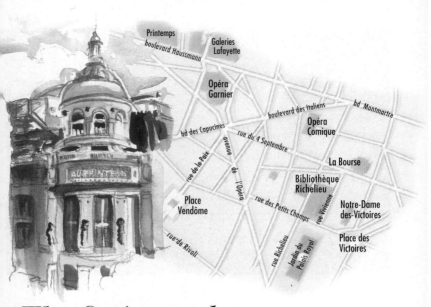

Printemps
boulevard Haussmann
Galeries Lafayette
Opéra Garnier
boulevard des Italiens
bd Montmartre
bd des Capucines
rue du 4 Septembre
Opéra Comique
rue de la Paix
avenue de l'Opéra
La Bourse
Bibliothèque Richelieu
Place Vendôme
rue des Petits Champs
rue Vivienne
Notre-Dame des-Victoires
rue de Rivoli
rue Richelieu
Jardin du Palais Royal
Place des Victoires

The Opéra and
the Grands Boulevards

In the 19th century, Haussmann's urban development project turned the Opéra district into a major centre of activity. With its department stores and impressive

The Palais Garnier is in the middle of one of Paris' most animated districts. Alongside banks and cinemas, large shops and boutiques display their enticing wares. The Café de la Paix on Boulevard des Capucines, offers a welcome place to rest.

boulevards, it is still animated by day though much quieter in the evening.

Avenue de l'Opéra epitomizes Haussmann's style.

The entire district stands in the shadow of the **Opéra Garnier,** named after its designer Charles Garnier. Construction work began in 1862 and the building was finally opened in 1875. This symbol of the Second Empire is a combination

The Palais Garnier. Above: The building is often likened to a huge wedding cake.
Left: Famous operas and ballets provided the inspiration for the ceiling paintings by Chagall.

of styles, from the classical to the baroque, typical of the style of the period of Napoleon III. Today, the building mainly stages ballets as most operas are now performed at the

A symphony in red and gold. The auditorium of the Opéra Garnier has five levels of boxes. The chandelier, weighing almost six tonnes, is suspended in the middle of a large dome supported by eight red and gold columns.

Chagall and the Opéra Garnier

One of the many names associated with the Opéra Garnier is that of Marc Chagall who painted the ceiling of the dome with scenes from nine operas and ballets including *Swan Lake, Romeo and Juliet* and the *Magic Flute*. The painter, engraver and sculptor was born in Russia in 1887, and arrived in Paris around 1910. He lived at 'La Ruche', a community of artists under the patronage of the sculptor Alfred Boucher, and associated with the likes of Apollinaire, Modigliani and Léger. By assimilating techniques from cubism to expressionism, he created his own style in which the intensity of the colours and the lyricism express the richness of his themes. Chagall died in Saint-Paul-de-Vence, France, in 1985.

Bastille. It boasts a dome, rotunda, colonnades and pediment, and houses many statues and busts of great composers. Outside, on the staircase leading to the main entrance, four groups symbolize Music, Lyrical Poetry, Lyrical Drama and Dance. The latter is a copy of Jean-Baptiste Carpeaux's masterpiece, now housed in the Musée d'Orsay, which was considered to be indecent and caused quite a scandal when it was first unveiled. Inside the Opéra is a magnificent staircase with volutes leading to the auditorium where the ceiling was decorated by the artist Marc Chagall.

The Parc Monceau, a leafy oasis laid out by the Duc de Chartres in 1778, has retained some of its original features, including this ornamental lake.

The arcades of Place Vendôme.

To the west of Boulevard Haussmann lies the Parc Monceau, an English-style garden designed in the 18th century by Carmontelle.

Rue de la Paix leads from the Opéra to **Place Vendôme,** designed by Hardouin-Mansart in 1698. The square's classical façades house the Ritz Hotel, banks and jewellery shops. In the centre of the square is the Colonne Vendôme (the Vendôme Column), on top of which sits a statue of Napoleon, commemorating his victory at Austerlitz.

Above: The statue of Guy de Maupassant in Parc Monceau.

The octagonal Place Vendôme was designed by Jules Hardouin-Mansart during the reign of Louis XIV. Today, in addition to the Ritz Hotel, banks, fashion houses and leading jewellery shops have also taken up residence under the arcades. A famous inhabitant, the composer Frédéric Chopin, died here in 1842, at No. 12.

The Jardin du Palais-Royal, surrounded by restaurants, art galleries and shops.

The revolutionary journalist, C a m i l l e D e s m o u l i n s , called the crowd to arms in front of the Café de Foy on July 12, 1789.

Right: The Palais-Royal's courtyard, with Buren's black-a n d - w h i t e striped columns.

Leave Place Vendôme via Rue Castiglione and walk along Rue de Rivoli to the **Palais-Royal**. The building is now home to the Conseil d'Etat (Council of State), the Ministère de la Culture (the Ministry for Culture) and the Conseil Constitutionnel (Constitutional Council). Its garden is now a haven of tranquillity, but over the years it has been a meeting place for prostitutes and a location for public debate.

The diameter given on the original plan of Place des Victoires was 256 feet (78 m).

The nearby **Place des Victoire**s, which was designed in the 17th century by Jules Hardouin-Mansart and dedicated to the Sun King, was Paris' first square in the shape of a circle. As a tribute to his ancestor, Louis XVIII commissioned Bosio to make the equestrian statue of Louis XIV which still stands in the square. Today, Paris' fashionable set shop at Cacharel, Thierry Mugler and Kenzo. The short Rue Vide-Gousset leads to the pretty Place des Petits-Pères whilst the Church of Notre-Dame-des-Victoires is still a place of devotion dedicated to the Virgin Mary.

Below: The shop window of the couturier Thierry Mugler on Place des Victoires, a centre of fashion and Parisian elegance. Other big names, such as Gaultier, can be found in the nearby Galerie Vivienne.

The dome of Sacré-Cœur at the top of Montmartre is the second-highest point in Paris after the Eiffel Tower.

Montmartre

From Place Pigalle to the steep slopes of Montmartre, Paris has become a world of entertainment. At the Moulin Rouge, sequins and feathers feature in its nightly

There is something of a village feel to Montmartre. The district is synonymous with painting and bohemian artists, but also has a thriving nightlife. Day and night, tourists come in their droves to appreciate its picturesque charms.

shows, while visitors throng to Place du Tertre for its artists and cafés.

The Basilica of Sacré-Cœur overlooks Montmartre.

Place du Tertre in the heart of Montmartre is an extremely colourful area where tourists and locals rub shoulders in the most bohemian of atmospheres. In what was once a 'free commune', founded during the 1871 insurrection against the

Alongside the Square Willette in the Halle Saint-Pierre, is the Museum of Naïve Art which houses publisher Max Fourny's fine collection of paintings and sculptures.

government (then resident at Versailles), the visitor can enjoy a drink at a bistro while listening to the old songs of Aristide Bruant accompanied on the accordion.

The tourist centre of Montmartre. Paintings on Place du Tertre, where artists paint portraits and landscapes, keeping the bohemian atmosphere alive.

Painting: like mother, like son

Suzanne Valadon (1865–1938) and her son Maurice Utrillo (1883–1955) are among those who epitomize the distinctive spirit of Montmartre. They both symbolize the bohemian life so well portrayed in Puccini's opera *La Bohème* (1896).

Suzanne Valadon, daughter of a laundry worker, was an acrobat before an accident ended her career. She then became a model for Renoir, Puvis de Chavanne, Toulouse-Lautrec and Degas. The latter encouraged her to become a painter, which she did, specializing in portraits, figures and nudes. Her son, Maurice Utrillo became an alcoholic at a very young age. As a form of therapy his mother encouraged his artistic flair, transforming him into a successful painter.

Strolling through Montmartre is rather like ambling through the winding streets of a hillside village, retracing the steps of famous artists and writers such as Toulouse-Lautrec, Renoir, Van Gogh, Gauguin, Cézanne, Utrillo, Valadon, Modigliani, Braque, Apollinaire and Picasso. Montmartre was also known for its vineyards, which still produce wine today. The **Sacré-Cœur**, a Romano-Byzantine basilica that took nearly 40 years to build (1876–1914), was only officially consecrated in 1919 at the end of World War I following the Allies' victory over the Central Powers.

Henri de Toulouse-Lautrec (1864–1901) drank and painted in Montmartre. His posters and portraits of La Goulue and Jane Avril helped to make him famous whilst immortalizing the district's cabarets.

The Moulin Rouge where dancers still perform the cancan at its nightly shows.

The Moulin de la Galette in Rue Lepic.

The façade of Au Lapin Agile, 22 Rue des Saules, a nightclub that was originally named the Cabaret des Assassins. A sign, painted at the end of the last century by the newspaper illustrator André Gill, depicting a rabbit jumping out of a saucepan, gave the place its current name ('Le Lapin de Gill' became 'Le Lapin Agile').

The districts of Montmartre and Pigalle have always been linked due to their bohemian character. A popular meeting place, visitors would rub shoulders with starving artists and ladies of the night without really mixing with them, coming instead to be entertained by cabarets and the singing street urchins, recorded by the illustrator Francisque Poulbot.

The tree-lined paths of Square Willette at the foot of Sacré-Coeur.

'Au Lapin Agile', Place des Abbesses, Rue de l'Abreuvoir and the Moulin de la Galette are just some associated with the evocative sites of Montmartre. The French cancan, introduced at the end of the 19th century, made the Moulin Rouge and its dancers such as Jane Avril, famous and provided inspiration for Toulouse-Lautrec.

Each year, around October, the Montmartre grape harvest takes place amid celebrations and entertainment, attracting both locals and curious onlookers. The Montmartre vineyard, reopened in 1933, produces annual vintages dedicated to famous people, such as the 1997 wine in tribute to Dalida, the popular singer who lived in the area.

The steel and glass buildings of La Villette display a highly technical style of architecture. Above: The Médiathèque (media library) rises above the moats.

A longside the historical city lies a more modern face of Paris in the shape of Bercy, La Villette and La Grande Arche de la Défense.

The Géode, a revolutionary cinema.

Futuristic Paris

The 21st century is fast approaching, and Paris, like all of the world's capital cities, is making serious preparations for it. The future, however, arrived in Paris a few years ago. The major building programme which has been implemented over the past two decades has filled Paris with buildings that are monuments to the forthcoming millennium. Stone, glass and steel combine to form enormous structures which dominate and enhance the city skyline, such as the Grande Arche de la Défense (opposite).

The Cité des Sciences: a veritable modern temple of learning.

The Follies, *cubes made out of concrete and red steel, are the work of Bernard Tschumi.*

The Cité des Sciences, which was designed by the architect Adrien Fainsilber, is based around the themes of

water, vegetation and light. The Zénith, a concert venue in the park, stages mainly rock concerts and can hold nearly 6000 people.

In north-east Paris, the abattoirs of La Villette have been replaced by a huge complex covering more than 125 acres (50 hectares). The **Cité des Sciences** (City of Science) is dedicated to technology and the **Cité de la Musique** (City of Music) to music. Visitors can also see a film in the spherical **Géode** cinema.

The Ministère des Finances.

The huge glass towers of the Bibliothèque Nationale de France resemble four giant books of knowledge.

No. 30, Place d'Italie is home to the Grand Ecran, one of the largest cinema screens in Paris.

To the east of Paris, the former wine market, between the Gare de Lyon and Quais de Bercy, has been replaced by the Ministère des Finances (Ministry of Finance) and the Palais Omnisports de Paris-Bercy (Paris-Bercy sports centre). On the other side of the Seine stands the new **Bibliothèque Nationale** (National Library).

The POPB (Palais Omnisports de Paris-Bercy) is a multi-purpose centre used to host the capital's major sporting and cultural events. The POPB's triangular and pyramid-shaped metal structures stretch over 20 acres (8 hectares) and are used for staging events from the French tennis open to rock concerts.

The world's largest companies, such as Elf and Total, are based in the skyscrapers of La Défense where the skyline resembles that of New York.

The Géode at La Villette and the Dôme Imax at La Défense are two Parisian cinemas capable of inciting physical sensations through audio-visual effects.

The Grande Arche de la Défense is 328 feet (100 metres) tall, and transforms the whole area into a futuristic city. Influenced by the New York sky-scrapers of Mies Van der Rohe, the architects erected glass and steel towers around the Grande Arche which contains a conference centre and art gallery.

A sculpture by Calder at La Défense.

The **Grande Arche de la Défense** stands to the west of Paris along the east-west thoroughfare that stretches from the Louvre, past Place de la Concorde and L'Etoile. The huge building is the work of the Danish architect Otto von Sprechelsenand and was completed in 1989. The surrounding district of La Défense is an ultra-modern business centre.

La Défense takes its name from the 1871 Prussian siege of Paris. The Grande Arche is an immense hollow cube offering 'an open window onto an unpredictable future'.

At the Chateau of Versailles, Louis XIV made no secret of his quest for power and eternal life. Magnificence and megalomania became the hallmarks of his reign.

L ouis XIV, the Sun King, chose Versailles as the site for a chateau worthy of the universe of which he intended to be the centre.

A detail from the Galerie des Glaces.

Versailles

The Château de Versailles is around 12 miles (20 km) west of Paris, and was built in the 17th century on the site of a former hunting lodge. This magnificent palace, built in accordance with the wishes and ambitions of King Louis XIV, is outstanding in every respect. The architecture, interior decor and superb gardens all combine to make the chateau a jewel of classical French art. Versailles was the capital of France, from the reign of the Sun King until the Revolution. Today, it is used mainly for large functions.

The Marble Courtyard at Versailles, decorated with marble busts.

In the 17th century, the royal residence of the Palais du Louvre became too small for the ambitions of Louis XIV and his large and demanding court. The Sun King decided to move to Versailles outside Paris, and construct a

This long sunny corridor with its arches is the perfect place in which to meditate, reminding us of the close links that once existed between Royal power and the Church.

sumptuous palace befitting his power and glory. He also hoped to indulge his passion for hunting whilst monitoring his rebellious and recalcitrant courtiers more effectively.

The baroque Chapelle Royale (Royal Chapel) at Versailles is a reminder that the Sun King was also very pious. Decorated with gold, the chapel symbolizes his dazzling power.

The Sun King

Of all the French kings, Louis XIV was perhaps the one who inspired most envy and admiration. Also known as Louis le Grand (Louis the Great), he was born in 1638 at Saint-Germain-en-Laye. As the grandson of Henri IV, son of Louis XIII and Anne d'Autriche, he ascended the throne at the age of five when his father died. Because he was too young to reign, the queen mother acted as regent with the help of Cardinal Mazarin, who founded the Bibliothèque Mazarine and the College des Quatre-Nations, the current Palais de l'Institut de France. The Sun King's lengthy 72-year reign was bathed in glory, and his greatest bequest to future generations was the beautiful Chateau of Versailles.

From 1668 onwards, Hardouin-Mansart and Le Vau were in charge of the giant building site that was to become the most beautiful palace in the world. It is true that the Sun King's megalomania was equalled only by his desire to please, seduce and impress his most humble subjects and princely guests alike. Hundreds of apartments, bedrooms, outbuildings and stables cover a vast space: the façade of the palace is 2231 feet (680 metres) long! The Galerie des Glaces (Hall of Mirrors), on the west side overlooking the gardens, is the palace's crowning glory.

The Galerie des Glaces with its mirrors and chandeliers is 230 feet (70 metres) long.

The equerries of King Louis XIV founded the Ecole d'Equitation Française (French Riding School) at Versailles.

The tall wide windows of the long Galerie des Glaces overlook the beautiful formal gardens.

The painter Charles le Brun dedicated his life to serving the king, with the sole aim of completing the luxurious interior decor demanded by Louis XIV for his palace. The 17 large mirrors in the Galerie des Glaces face the same number of windows, bathing the gallery in light. The Royal Apartments are next to the rooms dedicated to the gods of Olympus, including the Salon d'Apollon that was once the Throne Room.

Le Nôtre's geometric gardens have inspired many artists.

The king loved art, but was also passionate about nature. He had the Potager du Roi (King's Vegetable Garden) planted with various varieties of fruit and vegetables which still grow there today.

When Queen Marie-Thérèse died in 1683, the king turned the apartments into state rooms. He then left them to take up residence in the 'appartements du roi' (King's Apartments), closer to the south wing where the 'appartements de la reine' (Queen's Apartments) were occupied by Madame de Maintenon, his last mistress. After a secret marriage in 1685, they remained together until his death in 1715. It was under the Catholic influence of his new wife that Louis passed the Revocation of the Edict of Nantes, leading to the bloody persecution of Protestants.

During the storms of 1990, many trees and statues were damaged. Restoration work is still continuing.

Lavish spectacles were staged at Versailles, and today baroque music can still be heard in the Chapelle Royale.

One of the 300 statues in the park.

André Le Nôtre was at the height of his profession when he designed the Sun King's gardens. The latter loved well-ordered spaces, and sought to bring order to the universe through his gardens. The Parc de Versailles inspired the king to write *Manière de montrer les jardins de Versailles* (Methods of Landscaping the Gardens of Versailles).

Apollo, the Greek god of light and the sun, inspired Louis XIV, who named the gardens of Versailles, designed by Le Nôtre, after him. A clever mixture of classicism and the baroque, the lay-out of the park still inspires architects such as I. Ming Pei, who was responsible for designing the Louvre's glass pyramid.

One of the golden fountains commissioned by the Sun King.

The king also built the Pavillon du Grand Trianon, a superb building made of pink and white marble. His great-grandson, Louis XV, built the smaller Petit Trianon, thus completing the grandiose work of his ancestor. During the French Revolution, the royal family was finally ousted from the ravaged palace.

On three Sundays of each month, from May to September, the fountains opposite the Grand Canal are switched on, attracting visitors who come to picnic beside them on sunny summer days.
Legend has it that, on June evenings, a graceful but headless royal silhouette sometimes appears near the Temple de l'Amour. Could it be the ghost of Marie-Antoinette?

Creative Workshop

Having discovered the wonders of Paris, it's now time to get creative.

All you need are a few odds and ends and a little ingenuity to keep the spirit of your adventure alive by creating your own beautiful craft objects.

These simple yet ingenious ideas capture the special flavour of Paris and leave you with a permanent reminder of your visit.

An original, simple and fun way to preserve your holiday memories.

Feather Bracelet

*T*his fun wire
bracelet,
*simply decorated
with feathers and
beads, is inspired
by the stage
costumes of
dancing girls
from the Lido
in Paris.*

• Using piano cord, make
a circle 3" (7.5 cm) in
diameter.

• To close the bracelet,
create a double loop
around part of the circle,
twist each end around
the wire as shown in the
diagram, and close with
pliers.

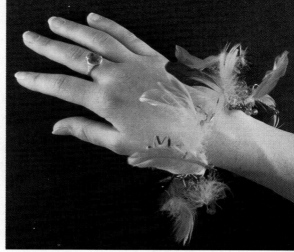

• Next, take the coloured wire and wind it around the piano cord circle.

• Make loops, twists and other shapes, threading beads along the length of the wire.

• Remember to use pliers to flatten the small blocking beads placed in front of and behind other beads to prevent them from slipping.

• Finally, insert the feathers into the loops, and flatten the loops with pliers to fix the feathers in place.

Materials

• 16" (40 cm) of piano cord • 1 reel of coloured wire • small, round, blue frosted-glass beads • oblong shiny beads, 0.2" (6 mm) long • small pieces of polished and pierced orange stone • several small blocking beads • 5 blue feathers • 8 orange feathers • 2 deep-red feathers • small pair of pliers

Painted Breakfast Bowl

B *righten up your breakfast bowls and bring a touch of France to your table... even if you decide to use them for cereal rather than coffee!*

• Using a 0.8" (2 cm) brush and red ceramic paint, paint the edge of the bowl, ensuring that the band of colour is the same width all the way round. The easiest way to do this is to use a brush that is the same width as you want the band to be.

• Use tracing paper to copy the lettering (opposite page) and then go over the letters on the back of the tracing paper using a soft pencil.

• Turn the tracing paper the right way up and position it on the bowl.

• Hold it in place with sticky tape and retrace the letters to transfer them onto the bowl.

• Using a very fine brush and ceramic paint, paint the letters with your hand raised as shown in the diagram.

To keep a steady hand, lean the hand holding the brush on the table. Then take the bowl in the other hand and turn it so that the inside is facing you.

Use the paint neat or slightly diluted, and do not take too much onto the brush at one time to avoid it from running.

Leave to dry.

café au lait

Materials

• 2 ceramic breakfast bowls • coloured ceramic paint • tracing paper • pencil • 0.8" (2 cm) brush • a fine brush • sticky tape

Bookmark

The design

• Draw a rectangle 6.3" x 2" (16 cm x 5 cm) onto a piece of stiff paper.

• In the centre of the rectangle, draw or trace the rose with a sharp pencil.

• Next, sketch a horizontal border at the top, and two perpendicular borders in the bottom right-hand corner 0.2" (5 mm) from the edge.

• Each border should be 0.2" (5 mm) wide and 1.6" (4 cm) long. 0.1" (3 mm) from the top border, draw a flap 0.4" (1 cm) deep using a dotted line.

Painting the rose

• First, paint the rose with a light Tyrian purple wash.

• Next, use the other reds and white to build up the rose, adding light and shade.

• Paint the leaves in a similar way using the green and white paints.

Painting the borders

• Inside the rectangles sketch small triangles

• Paint the triangles using olive green and Tyrian purple mixed

with white on each alternate triangle.
• Leave to dry.
• With a fine brush, paint white lines inside the green triangles and a white triangle inside each pink triangle.
• Then paint a smaller purple triangle in the centre of the white ones.
• Leave to dry.
• Complete by using a Stanley knife to cut the flap, following the dotted line.

Materials

• pencil • rubber• metal ruler
• set square • Stanley knife • sheet of thick eggshell or ivory-coloured paper
• sheet of tracing paper • fine paintbrush • poster paints in Tyrian purple, Persian red, China red, brown, olive green, white and willow green.

Boulangerie ShopWindow

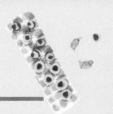

The boulangerie walls

• To construct the walls of the boulangerie, use a shoebox and cover the inside with stiff paper or fabric.

• First, cover the two long interior sides cutting the paper or fabric slightly longer than the size of the box so that the ends can be folded over onto the shorter sides.

• Then stick paper or fabric onto the two shorter sides (cut these to the exact size of the box) and to the back of the box.

• Cover the interior again with a second layer of paper or any other material that gives an impression of texture.

The loaves and cakes

• Use pastry to make the baguettes, ring-shaped loaves, croissants, tarts and puff pastries.

• Cut two other rectangles measuring 1.2" x 3.5" (3 cm x 9 cm) to make the boulangerie window displays. Make indents in them to create a baking tray effect.

• Cook all the items and leave to cool before painting them. • Once they are dry, stick the loaves and cakes onto the baking trays and the walls.

• Inside the boulangerie, make the trestles for the window displays using 4 pieces of cardboard measuring 3.5" x 2.4" (9 cm x 6 cm).

• Fold over the edge of one of the 2.4" (6 cm) sides by 0.4" (1 cm) and stick it to the ground.

• Fold over the second piece of cardboard in the same way and stick it 0.8" (2 cm) away from the first piece. Place the baking tray and pastries on top and stick in place.

• Make the second display in the same way

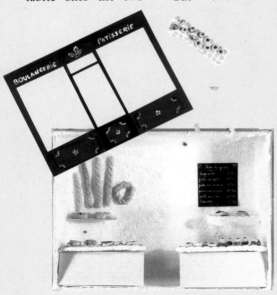

• To make the price list on the back wall, cut out a black cardboard rectangle measuring 1.8" x 1.6" (4.5 cm x 4 cm) and write the prices in white and gold ink.

The window display

• Use masking tape to attach plastic glass to the front of the box.
• Remove the sides of the shoebox lid, or use a rectangle of cardboard the same size as the box to make the window. The windows either side of the door measure 3" x 4.4" (8 cm x 11 cm). The edges of the doorframe are 0.2" (0.6 cm) wide. The door itself is a rectangle measuring 1.8" x 3.3" (4.5 cm x 8.5 cm), topped with another 1.8" x 0.5" (4.5 cm x 1.4 cm) rectangle.
• Paint the cardboard, frame and edges of the box. Attach the various items that make up the boulangerie window display.
• Close the box.

• Finally, glue the frame in place and attach a picture hook to the back of the box so that you can hang it on the wall.

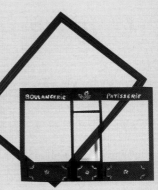

Materials

- shoebox • Stanley knife • metal ruler
- set square • glue • roll of masking tape
- black and white card • sheet of plastic glass (same size as the shoebox) • frame
- water-based paints in several colours
- black and gold ink • picture hook

Oeufs à la Neige

- Separate the egg whites and the yolks. Beat the egg whites into peaks and gradually add half the caster sugar.
- Bring 1.75 pints (1 litre) of water to the boil in a large saucepan.
- Place several dessertspoons of the egg white into the water when it is simmering, ensuring that they do not touch.
- Leave them to poach for two or three minutes and then turn them over.
- Next, use a slotted spoon to retrieve the egg whites

and drain them on a slightly sloping plate.
- Do this with all the egg whites and as soon as they are all cooked prepare the sauce.

Preparing the sauce

- Mix the five yolks with the remaining caster sugar, making a fairly clear runny paste.
- Pour some boiling milk on top, mix it into the eggs and pour it along with the remaining milk into a pan.
- Thicken the sauce on a low flame, stirring it and ensuring that it does not boil.

- Remove from the heat and stir it from time to time.
- Immediately before serving, add some Cointreau, orange essence or rose water to the sauce.
- Pour into bowls and place the egg whites on top. Garnish with orange peel and mint leaves.
Serve immediately.

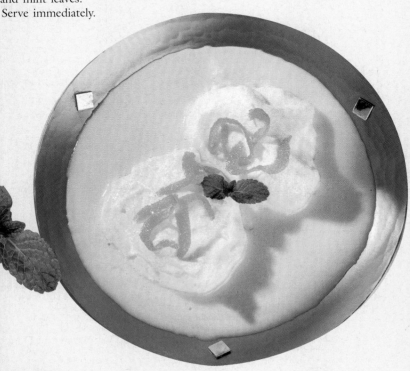

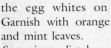

Ingredients

- 3 eggs • 4 oz (115 g) caster sugar • 2 yolks • 0.8 pints (450 ml) milk
- 2 tbsp Cointreau, rosewater or orange essence • 1 orange • fresh mint leaves.

INDEX

Acknowledgements

The publishers would like to thank all those who have contributed
to the preparation of this book, in particular:

Angie Allison, David Bême, Antoine Caron, Jean-Jacques Carreras,
Aude Desmortiers, Rupert Hasterok, Nicolas Lemaire, Hervé Levano,
Mike Mayor, Kha Luan Pham, Vincent Pompougnac,
Marie-Laure Ungemuth, Emmanuèle Zumstein.

Creative Workshop:
Jacqueline Damien (p. 136-137),
Michèle Forest (p. 132-133), Marie-Cécile Moreau (p. 138-139).

Translation: Patricia Clarke

Picture credits: Salamander Picture Library (p. 140-141).

Illustrations : Franz Rey, Valérie Zuber

Printed in Italy
Eurolitho — Milan
March 1999